From Zero To E-Commerce Hero

5 Steps to Multi-Million Success with $100

Abraham Wright

Contents

FORWARD

How To Build A Multi-Million Dollar Online Business In 5 Steps With Less Than $100 Per Month:

Within the ever-evolving e-commerce landscape, Abraham Wright's book, "From Zero To E-Commerce Hero," stands as a practical narrative for entrepreneurs seeking pragmatic insights. Abraham's own journey in the e-commerce industry gives insight to the foundational principles required for success in this highly competitive domain.

The book unveils a comprehensive blueprint, plain and simple, and is filled with actionable steps, enabling aspiring e-commerce entrepreneurs to attain multi-million-dollar success without the need for substantial capital.

These steps include identifying a profitable niche, establishing partnerships with local suppliers, creating a compelling online presence, mastering the art of pricing, and effectively navigating the intricacies of SEO and marketing strategies.

In a world where e-commerce success may appear elusive, this book offers a narrative that's both relatable and practical, guiding entrepreneurs towards a path that leads from **Zero to E-Commerce Hero.**

Disclaimer:

The purpose of the content that is offered in this book is to provide insightful and informative material on the various themes that are covered. Any and all numerical figures included in this book are merely illustrative and have no other purpose than to support the author's theoretical arguments.

The publisher and the author are not liable for any potential damages or adverse consequences that may arise from actions or lack thereof by individuals who read or follow the information that is provided in this book. Neither party can be held responsible for any actions taken or not taken as a result of reading this book.

The references that are provided in this book are there for the sole purpose of providing information; they are not intended to be taken as recommendations of certain websites or other sources. The reader should also be informed that the websites that are referenced in this book may, over the course of time, go through modifications or become irrelevant.

Introduction

A great number of people have the goal of achieving financial independence, with the goal being able to break free from the constraints of traditional 9 to 5 blue-collar work routines, in which the stress of living paycheck to paycheck can impede personal development. The journey toward monetary autonomy typically starts with the conception of an idea and calls for hard work that is both focused and consistent. Focus is one of the most important factors that will determine how successful this venture is.

To keep one's concentration implies to rid oneself of any and all unneeded distractions that could draw one's attention away from the target they have set for themselves. In this book, I will give a blueprint that has been successful for a number of individuals; a blueprint that enables you to embark on a multi-million dollar business adventure with an investment of less than $100. I will present this blueprint so that you can take advantage of its potential. This strategy is one of the business endeavors I've come across that has the least amount of risk possible, and it is certainly doable. In order to get started on this adventure, all that is required is access to a computer and the internet.

The actions that are outlined in this blueprint are easy to understand and basic to carry out. Once you have determined your specialty and found a provider, the workload is actually quite feasible, and you may even be able to delegate certain responsibilities to a free agent. This is a tried-and-true strategy that can put you on the right track toward reaching your goal of being financially independent.

Step 1: Identifying a Niche

Determining a business niche is an intricate and multifaceted undertaking that necessitates rigorous research, strategic deliberation, and an extensive comprehension of the intended consumer base. Entrepreneurs are required to identify unfulfilled needs or underutilized sectors within an industry and customize their offerings to cater to those distinct desires.

The journey begins with a thorough market investigation. Venture capitalists are required to analyze the broader industrial environment to identify trends, voids, and opportunities. Conducting research on competitors, customer behaviors, and emergent technologies or advancements is recommended.

A thriving niche frequently corresponds with the entrepreneur's area of interest and proficiency. Those who are sincerely enthusiastic about the subject matter are more inclined to maintain dedication and foster innovation. As a result, they ought to engage in introspection and determine which industries or subjects authentically captivate their interest.

It is crucial to refine the intended audience. Entrepreneurs ought to develop comprehensive consumer personas in order to gain insight into the demographics, preferences, and challenges faced by their prospective clientele. This enables services or products to be tailored to satisfy particular requirements.

It is essential to comprehend the competitive landscape. Entrepreneurs ought to evaluate the merits and demerits of current participants within the selected market segment. This can facilitate the identification of domains in which they possess exceptional capabilities or can provide a distinctive value proposition.

It is advisable to conduct thorough validation of a business concept prior to making a complete investment in a niche. To obtain feedback, this may be achieved via focus groups, surveys, or even by offering a minimum viable product (MVP) to a select group of prospective consumers.

After the establishment of the company, proprietors ought to consistently evaluate and refine their offerings in accordance with client input. This guarantees that the products or services adapt in order to satisfy the evolving demands of the niche market.

Prior to carving out a niche, a solid brand presence must be established. A unique brand identity, message, and narrative may assist a business in differentiating itself and establishing a more profound connection with its target market.

Effective content marketing is critical for connecting with and influencing a specific target audience. Producing instructional, pertinent, and high-quality content can assist a business in establishing itself as an industry authority and attracting new customers.

Developing relationships within the niche community may result in opportunities for partnership and collaboration. This could potentially facilitate the organization in expanding its audience and establishing its credibility.

Finally, vigilance and flexibility are essential qualities. Competition, market conditions, and consumer preferences are all susceptible to modification. Entrepreneurs must remain vigilant regarding these trends and be prepared to adapt their strategies in response.

Exploring a business niche necessitates an ongoing and dynamic procedure that combines a combination of in-depth knowledge, enthusiasm, flexibility, and significant research into the intended market. The crux of the matter is identifying unfulfilled needs and developing specialized solutions that appeal to a specific clientele, thereby fostering business expansion and prosperity.

It is essential to identify a niche that aligns with your individual preferences and capabilities. If you have a strong passion or interest in art, you should investigate niches within the discipline. In the same way, individuals with programming expertise or a propensity for technology should prioritize segments that are in close proximity to their area of expertise.

The rationale for selecting a field of expertise that aligns with one's personal interests and capabilities is to enable one to wholeheartedly dedicate oneself to and thrive in entrepreneurial pursuits. You will naturally devote a significant portion of your energy and enthusiasm to the expansion of your business, thereby increasing its likelihood of success.

Although it is possible to venture into niches unrelated to your expertise or interests, doing so can become progressively more difficult as your business grows.

During the Gold Rush period, when Levi Strauss first set out to establish a denim business in the United States, he discerned a distinct and advantageous market niche. Prior to that time, the majority of individuals and businesses were occupied with providing prospectors with mining tools and apparatus, such as shovels and maps. Unexpectedly, there was a lack of attention given to the significance of developing suitable work attire for the miners engaged in mining activities.

Levi Strauss demonstrated exceptional foresight by devising a solution: producing pants made from resilient fabric that are both functional and aesthetically appealing. Unbeknownst to him at the time, this ground-breaking uniform would progress to become one of the most recognizable fashion icons of the twenty-first century. Even more astounding is the fact that Levi's trousers persisted in the face of obsolescence long after the Gold Rush concluded. Conversely, they persevered and have maintained their success to the present day, evolving into an internationally renowned and enduring apparel and denim brand.

Similar to the success of Levi Strauss, it is imperative to identify one's niche prior to undertaking an entrepreneurial endeavor. It is highly recommended to select a niche in which your intended products are comparatively small in size and weight, especially if your objective is to establish a prosperous online enterprise. It is advisable for a start-up to strive for efficient management of shipping expenses and capitalize on uncomplicated logistics alternatives, such as small shipping companies and postal services.

Although it is not unfeasible to begin with bulky or heavy products, the market generally prefers items that are straightforward to dispatch. Vanities and commodities are examples of products that typically acquire traction more rapidly in the online business environment. Nevertheless, avoid prematurely becoming preoccupied with the product's dimensions, volume, or weight. Defining and identifying your niche should be your principal objective. After identifying your niche, it becomes easier to determine which products are most suitable for your online enterprise.

It is critical to develop a comprehensive business road map that addresses all aspects, including product selection, marketing, and sales strategies. One benefit of this business model is that it obviates the necessity of product ownership or wholesale procurement. Furthermore, there is no requirement for tangible inventory storage space, as one can utilize the inventory of a supplier in order to fulfill customer demands.

Utilizing the MAGIC formula as a compass to locate your niche is possible. MAGIC, which stands for Cash-flow, Innovation, Awesomeness, Greatness, and Money, are all essential elements that your niche should include. Let us explore the following facets:

It should be possible for the niche you select to produce a profit. Assess this by analyzing the financial components. What is the annual sales revenue, measured in millions or billions of dollars, that products within your niche produce? Conduct an analysis of the trends; are these figures increasing or decreasing? Money is a telling indicator of the viability of your niche.

Consider whether the products in your niche are genuinely phenomenal. Will consumers perceive them as appealing and persuasive to the extent that they warrant a purchase? Do these products possess authentic excellence and the ability to enhance the customer's life? Always keep in mind that clients are purchasing something of value in exchange for their money.

The concept of greatness pertains to the value that your products provide. They should be distinctive and fulfill a function that strongly appeals to the intended recipients. Customers are willing to invest in an exceptional product because it effectively satisfies their requirements or resolves their problems.

Innovation is a transformative force. Your niche should, like the moment Steve Jobs unveiled the iPhone, contain innovative components that have the potential to disrupt the market or revolutionize an industry. Innovative products possess the capacity to captivate consumers' attention and establish an enduring influence.

Establishing a sustainable cash flow is critical. Companies must rapidly generate revenue. Potential investors may be deterred from investing even if you have a brilliant concept or product if the return on investment takes years to materialize. Individuals prefer to obtain returns on their investments as quickly as possible. A solid business strategy ought to guarantee a rapid accumulation of cash flow.

The transmission of messages via channels that can reach a broad audience is a fundamental principle in marketing. For example, a message such as "America is great" imprinted on the one-dollar bill or another widely used piece of currency has the potential to reach millions of individuals. Likewise, your niche should possess the capacity to engage and connect with a wide-ranging audience. In conclusion, the MAGIC formula can assist you in identifying a market segment that possesses not only financial potential but also customer interest, value proposition, innovation, and a steady cash flow, thereby adhering to the tenets of prosperous business enterprises. It is imperative to contemplate a market niche that provides a wide variety of products. The greater the variety offered by a niche, the greater the likelihood of achieving effective sales. Although it is feasible to establish a niche revolving around a solitary product, it is critical that the product adheres to the MAGIC formula and exhibits distinctive and pioneering attributes.

As an illustration, upon commencing my enterprise, I sold Oregano oil procured exclusively from a supplier. In the beginning, the product offering was solitary. Nevertheless, as a novel product, Oregano oil continued to attract a steady increase in demand from consumers.

My product line was gradually diversified to incorporate an assortment of essential oils. Subsequently, I formed a strategic alliance with a wholesaler, which enabled me to provide my clientele with an expanded selection of products without incurring the expense of inventory management. I earned a commission by acting as an intermediary and marketing the wholesaler's products.

The crux of the matter is that a niche containing a diverse range of products is frequently more beneficial. The requirements of individuals are varied, and the functioning of commerce is governed by the principles of probability. In comparison to a niche with a single product offering, expanding your customer base and attaining success are enhanced by providing multiple products.

Step 2: Finding a Local Supplier

This step discusses identifying a local supplier for your niche with a moderate to substantial inventory.

The following course of action, after identifying your niche, is to locate an appropriate supplier. While it is possible for your supplier to be local or international, we will concentrate on local suppliers with inventory for the purposes of this discussion.

The distribution business model, frequently employed by international suppliers, presents an intriguing and potentially lucrative opportunity. Nonetheless, it presents its own array of difficulties. Although it provides the possibility of generating passive income, its management can be quite complex. You may find it challenging to resolve consumer issues when you do not have direct access to the products in question. Difficulties may arise when attempting to provide customer service and resolve issues under an outsourcing model.

Working with local suppliers who manage their own inventory and provide greater direct control and involvement in business operations will be the focus of this book.

The central idea at hand pertains to the establishment of a prosperous online enterprise requiring little capital outlay, restricted exposure to risk, and the possibility of substantial financial gains. At the core of this framework resides the function of your supplier, who serves as your inventory holder in essence. This method eliminates the requirement for the maintenance of a tangible inventory of products. Conversely, you function as an intermediary, capitalizing on the value and revenue generated by your supplier's products. You and your supplier both gain from this symbiotic relationship, as you act as a sales channel and obtain a portion of the proceeds. Profit margins and other particulars pertaining to this partnership will be thoroughly examined in the subsequent discussion on pricing strategies.

This business paradigm is elegant due to its versatility and adaptability. The composition of your suppliers may differ in accordance with the characteristics of your industry niche and your particular business goals. They may include service providers, artisanal boutiques, manufacturers, wholesalers, or traditional retailers. Your niche is closely reflected in the supplier selection process, which allows you to tailor your business to the specific requirements and attributes of your selected market.

By forming alliances with these suppliers, you gain access to an array of benefits. Listed below are several important benefits:

Minimal Financial Risk:

The absence of investment obligations pertaining to inventory procurement and storage substantially lessens one's financial risk. By reducing the entry barrier for aspiring entrepreneurs, the potential loss in the event that the business fails to gain traction as anticipated is mitigated.

Cost-Effectiveness:

It is possible to run your business with minimal administrative expenses. No warehousing, storage facility, or the associated costs are required. This cost-effectiveness increases the potential for profit.

Offering Diverse Products:

By leveraging the varied inventories of your suppliers, you gain the ability to provide an extensive selection of products or services that effectively address the varied demands of your target demographic. Through diversification, a greater number of customers may be attracted.

Prioritize Sales and Marketing:

The central emphasis of your endeavors should be on sales and marketing. Without being weighed down by inventory management, you can focus on effectively promoting your products or services, developing your brand, and expanding your customer base.

Capitalizing on Expertise:

Suppliers frequently possess extensive knowledge and expertise pertaining to their specific domains. You can refine your offerings, obtain access to high-quality products, and gain valuable insights by leveraging their experience.

Scalability:

You can easily extend your business as it expands by establishing alliances with supplementary suppliers or broadening your assortment of products and services. Scalability enables swift expansion while circumventing the logistical intricacies that plague conventional enterprises.

Fundamentally, this business model capitalizes on the advantages of specialization and collaboration, enabling you to concentrate on your core competencies—establishing connections with consumers, promoting products, and generating revenue.

It is a mutually beneficial ecosystem in which both you and your suppliers can flourish; this is a win-win situation. We shall further examine multiple facets of this business model, such as pricing strategies, customer engagement, and scaling to ensure long-term success.

Suppose that you have selected the jewelry industry as your online business niche. At this juncture, it is opportune to locate a reliable jewelry supplier with the capacity to offer an extensive variety of products. The procedure commences with the establishment of rapport with prospective suppliers. It is possible to visit them, participate in substantive dialogues, and request a copy of their product catalog. This in-person exchange enables you to determine their credibility and evaluate the assortment of jewelry they provide.

It is advisable to inquire about their most popular products during your discussions. A comprehension of their most sought-after products can assist in coordinating inventory decisions with market demand. Additionally, invest time in investigating the supplier's website if it has a digital presence. By accessing their products through this digital portal, one can gain significant knowledge regarding the scope of their stock and identify particular jewelry items that may be suitable for inclusion in an online store.

Through thorough examination of the supplier's catalog and online presence, one will acquire the necessary knowledge to make well-informed decisions regarding the products that should be showcased in the jewelry niche. This research phase ensures that your online business satisfies the desires and requirements of your target market and lays the groundwork for a prosperous partnership.

The task of identifying the most reliable supplier necessitates comprehensive investigation and scrupulousness. The supplier can be likened to a priceless gem discovered during an entrepreneurial expedition. Establishing trust and maintaining regularity, especially during the initial phases, are contingent upon forming alliances with dependable suppliers. As a result, initiating the supplier search is a crucial undertaking.

In order to identify the optimal supplier, it is necessary to perform meticulous research. For instance, when embarking on a business venture such as nutritional supplements sales, it is critical to discern the most esteemed retailers operating within the sector. The success of your company is contingent on the dependability and quality of your supplier.

To initiate your inquiry, investigate multiple pathways. Hire Google to locate prospective vendors who are in line with your area of expertise. Examine periodicals for mentions of industry executives. Inquire with the Chamber of Commerce in your area regarding the industry's leading companies. To identify suppliers and retailers who specialize in your niche, consult the Yellow Pages. The significance of soliciting recommendations from acquaintances and peers, who may possess valuable insights, should not be underestimated.

A crucial step in the establishment of a business is ensuring that a supplier provides a physical inventory that is readily available for use. Failure to consider this pivotal element may hinder your advancement and impede your trajectory towards achievement. As a result, invest the time and energy required to systematically identify and establish a collaborative relationship with a dependable supplier, as this serves as the fundamental pillar of your entrepreneurial endeavor.

After effectively securing a dependable supplier, the subsequent critical undertaking is to commence the process of catalog construction. This procedure entails the discerning selection of products to be sold within a specific niche, followed by arranging your products into an all-encompassing catalog. To optimize this undertaking, contemplate utilizing a spreadsheet application such as Excel or Google Sheets.

Every product in this catalog merits an elaborate description. Pretending the rationale behind consumers' desire to acquire a specific product is of the utmost importance. Make an additional effort to improve the description of the product in order to increase its allure, if one already exists. Customers are frequently unaware of the existence or utility of particular products; therefore, it is your responsibility to inform them.

Bear in mind that as you develop your catalog, it will function as a valuable reference when you commence the construction of your website. Developing thorough descriptions serves the dual purpose of enlightening prospective purchasers and aiding in the domain of search engine optimization (SEO). Having a catalog that is well-organized and contains the appropriate keywords will increase the visibility and prominence of your website in online searches.

Moreover, through the creation of this catalog, you are effectively establishing your virtual inventory – an invaluable collection of products that you have not invested a single dollar in procuring. Your action is required to present this inventory to the world and transform it into commerce. It is comparable to unearthing a personal treasure on Alibaba, ripe with untapped potential that is anxious to be exploited and presented to satisfied clientele.

It is important to understand that the process of locating a supplier does not require one to be the only one. Indeed, you possess the prerogative to establish partnerships with an unlimited number of suppliers, on the condition that they satisfy the standards of dependability and uphold a tangible stock. Consider that you have decided to specialize in the sale of infant products. In the given situation, one may procure inventory from Supplier X while simultaneously investigating offerings from Supplier Y. This strategy enables the expansion of the product catalog, thereby providing customers with a greater variety of choices.

Occasionally, it may come to your attention that both Supplier X and Supplier Y offer the identical product, denoted as Product P. In such situations, calculate your profit margin by calculating the average price of Product P from both vendors. This methodology guarantees pricing competitiveness without compromising the ability to generate revenue.

The transportation suitability of a product is an additional critical factor to contemplate when constructing a virtual inventory. Certain items, such as combustible materials or air compressors, may present difficulties or even legal constraints in terms of air transportation.

Adherence to shipping regulations and awareness of these limitations are of utmost importance.

Bear in mind that your online inventory is akin to a wealth of potential resources that are just waiting to be exploited. Make an endeavor to construct, improve, and expand it. Placing quality above quantity is of utmost importance; overstocking your inventory would compromise the quality of your products.

Achieving a sustainable and dependable business is of paramount importance, necessitating the maintenance of a balanced approach that safeguards the interests of customers and the prosperity of the enterprise.

After successfully identifying niche-aligned suppliers for your inventory, it is critical to institute structure into your business operations. An efficient method of accomplishing this is by aggregating all of your product information into a CSV (Comma-Separated Values) file or, alternatively, a well-structured spreadsheet.

The implementation of CSV files can significantly optimize the procedure when one resolves to convert their enterprise to an e-commerce platform.

CSV file creation is simplified by a variety of software alternatives, including free and open-source programs. Having utilized e-commerce platforms such as Shopify or GoDaddy, these CSV files will be of the utmost importance. They revolutionize the process of establishing an online store by streamlining its operations.

Website development, which previously required three to six months, can now be completed in one to two weeks, or even sooner, contingent on the level of effort and time devoted to the construction of the site.

Step 3: Building or Cloning an E-Commerce Site

In this step we will discuss building an e-commerce website by creating your online store or replicating an existing one.

With the advent of user-friendly tools and modern technology, creating a website has evolved from a once-difficult task to one of the most straightforward methods of establishing an online presence.

A decade ago, constructing an e-commerce platform was a difficult and expensive undertaking. One can now establish an e-commerce website, despite lacking significant technological expertise. Alternatively, you can outsource the task to a freelancer; however, this may incur expenses ranging from $100 to $1000, contingent upon the particular specifications you have in relation to platforms such as GoDaddy or Shopify.

With a fundamental understanding of computers and the internet, creating a website does not pose an excessively difficult undertaking.

Domain Name:

You will require a domain name for your website to get started. It is essential to choose a memorable and appealing domain name, as this will increase the discoverability of your website when Google indexes it for Google Analytics. A memorable name is an asset to one's marketing efforts. Who could forget domain names such as business.com or amazon.com?

Unbelievably, the domain name business.com was sold for a substantial sum of one million dollars, exclusive of any accompanying website.

Commence the process of developing your website by conducting a domain name search for a memorable and succinct name that accurately reflects your area of expertise. Ensure that it is succinct, captivating, and noteworthy. After locating the ideal name, verify its availability to ensure it is available for purchase. The annual cost of registering a domain name ranges from $9.99 to $15. Hostinger and GoDaddy are among the many companies that offer domain name registrations.

Shopify, a platform widely recognized for its intuitive e-commerce website development features, also offers the option to register a domain name. In addition to its competitors, GoDaddy provides a more economical and competitive e-commerce builder than Shopify. These e-commerce platforms eliminate the necessity for coding or programming expertise in order to facilitate the creation of websites.

E-Commerce Platforms:

After obtaining a domain name for your online enterprise, you can proceed with the development of your e-commerce website. There are three simple approaches to establishing an electronic commerce website, with the most straightforward being the utilization of a pre-built platform such as Shopify. This hassle-free platform grants you the autonomy to efficiently and expeditiously develop your e-commerce website.

Comma-Separated Values (CSV) File:

Simply import the Comma-Separated Values (CSV) file that you have created into the platform. For this reason, in Step 2, I emphasized the significance of constructing a well-organized inventory catalog. The establishment of this catalog will substantially streamline the process of developing your online enterprise, as Shopify assumes the majority of the labor-intensive tasks. Your principal responsibility entails adding your products to your website.

For those who are not acquainted with the phrase "exporting," it denotes the process of transferring data from one location or format to another, such as your product information contained in a CSV file.

Exporting, as it pertains to this context, entails transferring the information from your inventory catalog to the Shopify platform, thereby facilitating the seamless integration of your products onto your e-commerce website. By employing this streamlined approach, you can effectively allocate time and energy towards constructing your online store.

If your website contains a relatively small number of products, it may be unnecessary to generate a CSV file; you can enter the items manually. Shopify provides a one-month free trial, during which you have sufficient time to manually add or import all of your products from the CSV file. In a similar fashion, GoDaddy's e-commerce platform offers a complimentary trial period in which products can be configured.

OpenCart is an additional economical alternative to Shopify and GoDaddy. OpenCart is an e-commerce platform that enables the development of open-source purchasing websites. Payment for hosting is the only requirement; prices vary from $2.99 to $30 per month, contingent upon the user's data consumption requirements. I would like to suggest Shopify, as their hosting is included in their monthly plan. After a one-month free trial, their most affordable plan costs $51 per month after the initial three months are billed at $1 per month.

Initially, an expensive plan may not be essential; one may opt to upgrade as sales volume progresses. Additionally, GoDaddy is a budget-friendly option.

Shop Themes:

It is essential, prior to beginning the development of your website, to choose an appropriate theme for your store. There are a variety of themes available for your niche, some of which are free and others of which may demand payment. Numerous complimentary themes are more than adequate for a website.

Shopify provides an integrated payment system for payment processing, which necessitates the linking of your financial information to your website. Solutions are also provided by Shopify with regard to logistics. The integration of both national and private carriers into the Shopify platform is seamless, mirroring the integration of GoDaddy. On the contrary, in the case of OpenCart, acquiring an API key or code to integrate their systems into your e-commerce platform requires you to initiate communication with carriers.

Both GoDaddy and Shopify provide the option to employ their own specialists to aid in the development of your website. We will not, however, delve into these services, as the concentration of this book is on establishing a successful business with a $50 investment. Conversely, you may wish to employ freelancers from alternative platforms, such as GoDaddy or Shopify, who frequently provide more competitive rates and may possess substantial expertise in website development.

Although Shopify and GoDaddy are commendable alternatives, it is important to acknowledge that there are other viable choices as well. Certain enterprises choose to utilize the WooCommerce platform, especially if they possess prior experience in developing WordPress websites. By integrating seamlessly with WordPress themes, WooCommerce provides an additional feasible option for the development of an e-commerce website.

It is crucial to bear in mind that the process of developing an e-commerce website has become extraordinarily convenient in the current digital environment. Maintaining concentration and opting for the platform that corresponds to one's proficiency and level of ease are crucial. If you possess prior experience in developing WordPress websites, WooCommerce may prove to be an excellent choice.

Cloning:

There is a shrewd opportunity to rapidly duplicate an established e-commerce website owned by your supplier through the process of replicating it. Through the utilization of web harvesting software, one can effectively produce a CSV file comprising all the requisite information. This file can subsequently be exported to an independent e-commerce platform. Let us contemplate a situation in which your supplier maintains a comprehensive online catalog featuring more than one thousand products. By utilizing a web scraper, one can effortlessly extract this data and construct their inventory.

Although lacking legal expertise, it is generally permissible to utilize software such as web scrapers for this particular objective. To inject some creativity into your website, you may subsequently revise the product descriptions utilizing Quillbot or other complimentary resources.

One benefit of utilizing web scrapers is the ability to rapidly develop an e-commerce website, even if the site contains a substantial quantity of products, potentially reaching millions. Upon the conclusion of the extraction procedure and the generation of the CSV file, a straightforward export to the preferred e-commerce platform (e.g., Shopify, GoDaddy, OpenCart, etc.) is all that is required. Your website is now operational.

Establishing an online boutique to exhibit specialized products to a potentially vast consumer base of millions or billions is the overarching objective, regardless of whether one opts to develop a custom website or replicate an existing one. This is the internet's enchantment: it provides an extraordinary marketing opportunity.

Prominent e-commerce enterprises such as Shein, which debuted as a modest online boutique specializing in wedding gowns, and Amazon, which originated in a garage, expanded rapidly into multibillion-dollar sectors. You currently possess the same opportunity at your disposal due to the internet.

Obtaining what previously demanded hundreds of thousands of dollars in loans and funding for businesses can now be accomplished for as little as $51 per month, contingent upon the e-commerce platform selected. Due to the affordability and accessibility of online business ventures, aspiring entrepreneurs can now reach a worldwide audience with minimal financial outlay.

These e-commerce platforms offer forums and video tutorials that make learning how to set up your website a straightforward process, even if you initially feel overwhelmed. It's important to keep in mind that the best way to overcome challenges is to tackle them head-on and persevere.

As soon as you have finished the creation of your website, it is of the utmost importance to check to see that it has correct descriptions and information that is exhaustive regarding your company.

"About Us"

When customers go to your web platform, they should quickly be able to determine who you are, how to get in touch with you, and the backstory of your company. You should pay particular attention to the "About Us" area of your website, since this is the place where you may present information regarding the background, values, and goals of your company.

Your website's trust will increase as a direct result of your demonstrated openness and transparency.

It is important to keep in mind that the fact that your company operates in the virtual environment is not a reason to keep its operations hidden from the public eye.

Instead, you should make it a priority to be open and honest with your customers regarding your company in order to earn their trust.

Registering Your Business:

You should also give some thought to the importance of registering your company formally. In the beginning phases of your business, this might not be a top priority for you.

This is especially true when you consider that you might not have any tax debt in the first year if your company hasn't reached a certain income threshold.

Tax Considerations:

On the other hand, as soon as your company begins to develop traction, it is absolutely necessary to register it and get a tax identification number.

When you work with an accountant or deal with other tax-related issues in the future, this step will prove to be a very helpful resource.

Step 4: Getting the Price Right:

In this step we will discuss a Pricing Strategy, and learn how to set competitive and profitable prices.

Pricing is an essential determinant of your company's profitability. It is crucial to bear in mind that the objective is to establish a profitable enterprise, not a philanthropic one, which necessitates a minimal financial investment and an almost nonexistent degree of risk.

Consequently, it is critical to establish appropriate prices for your products. Your pricing strategy should be in accordance with your intended profit margins, the number and variety of products you offer, and your niche.

It is particularly critical to avoid overinflating prices when a supplier offers identical products for sale online. It is essential to strike an equilibrium between profitability and competitiveness.

For instance, suppose you procure 20 units of Product X from your supplier at a cost of $6 each, and you generate monthly sales of this quantity. It would be more prudent to resell them for $5 as opposed to charging $8. You will generate a $40 profit per product sold in this manner.

Excessive price inflation could potentially restrict monthly sales to five items, yielding a profit per product of $20 rather than the intended $40.

The crucial factor is to commence gradually and consistently. Instead of worrying about the speed at which you will begin to see profits, concentrate on maintaining consistency.

A French proverb states, "Appetite comes with eating."

Partnering with Suppliers:

As your enterprise expands, you may consider exploring potential partnerships with suppliers other than your current one, which could further enhance your profit margins. Therefore, to ensure the success of your business, prioritize low-risk operations, consistent sales, and efficient marketing strategies.

Likewise, the potential profit margin differs based on the niche product. Let us consider an instance where one makes the decision to specialize in the sale of jewelry products, having discerned their niche and located a dependable supplier. When this occurs, products such as a gold pendant can generate substantial profit margins.

For example, if the ring is priced at $500 by your supplier, it is conceivable that you could resell it on your website for a range of $600 to $800. This is not inherently price inflation, as jewelry frequently possesses intrinsic value and offers substantially higher profit margins than other product categories.

Conversely, in the context of selling children's toys, if a specific toy (referred to as Toy A) is offered by your supplier for $80, you may not be permitted to mark it up on your website by more than $100. As niche and market dynamics play a significant role, there is no universal formula for determining product prices. Striking a balance between competitive pricing and profitability is of utmost importance in the context of one's particular industry.

Profit Margins:

When you're dealing with a large inventory of products, like in the case of selling beauty products with over 2000 items from your suppliers, setting prices can be simplified using a percentage-based margin approach. One effective method is to apply a fixed profit margin percentage to each product's cost. For instance, you might decide on a 15% profit margin to be added to the cost price of each item.

Leveraging tools like a CSV sheet and spreadsheet software like Excel, you can efficiently apply this margin formula to all your products. This simplifies the pricing process significantly, allowing you to swiftly determine the selling price for each item in your inventory.

By using a consistent percentage-based margin across your entire range of products, you not only streamline your pricing strategy but also ensure that your pricing remains competitive and aligned with your profit goals. It's an efficient way to maintain pricing consistency while managing a large and diverse product catalog.

Pricing beauty products, which typically consist of more than 2,000 items sourced from suppliers, can be more easily managed through the implementation of a percentage-based margin strategy. Implementing a fixed profit margin percentage on the cost of each product is an effective approach. For example, one might establish a 15% profit margin which would be appended to the item's cost pricing.

Spreadsheet Software:

By utilizing spreadsheet software such as Excel and CSV sheets, one can effectively implement this margin formula across all products. This greatly streamlines the pricing procedure, enabling you to efficiently ascertain the selling price for every item in your stock.

By applying a uniform percentage-based margin to your entire product line, you ensure that your prices remain competitive and in accordance with your profit objectives, while also streamlining your pricing strategy. While overseeing a vast and varied assortment of products, this method effectively ensures pricing uniformity.

Over time, as you gain insights into your product performance, you can make informed decisions about adjusting prices.

For example, let's say you have a best-selling product, Product X, and you consistently sell 1000 units of it each month. Upon analysis, you discover that by offering coupons or implementing discounts, the sales of this product could potentially increase to 8 to 10 times its current volume.

In such a scenario, it becomes a logical choice to reduce the price of Product X to tap into this increased demand and boost sales significantly.

For valuable insights into crafting an effective pricing strategy, I recommend exploring the books authored by Alex Hormozi.

Step 5: SEO and Marketing Strategies

As this guide draws to a close, it is crucial to emphasize that the establishment of an e-commerce enterprise is merely the start.

Although your website may be operational and accepting orders, it is still necessary to ensure that it is discoverable and visible in order to generate sales.

Search engine optimization (SEO) is a significant factor in this context. You can considerably enhance the likelihood of achieving a high ranking in Google search results by judiciously integrating keywords into the meta-tags and descriptions of your website.

Keywords:

Upon a user entering a keyword associated with your products, the likelihood of your website being displayed in the search results increases.

For SEO success, the precise positioning of meta tags and descriptions is critical. Moreover, Shopify provides a practical artificial intelligence (AI) instrument that can aid in the creation of meta descriptions. A few rudimentary words are all that is required for this artificial intelligence tool to generate captivating descriptions.

Images of your products in high quality are of equal importance. You will need to obtain images from the internet or the suppliers of your suppliers if they are not provided by yours. It is virtually impossible to sell a product online without an accompanying image, given the critical role that visuals play in attracting and engaging potential customers.

Dropshipping:

When one is engaged in drop-shipping, introducing a new product, or establishing an online presence for a physical store, they encounter a substantial quandary: how can one guarantee that consumers are able to locate the online store?

Those who discover your e-commerce platform via a search engine are generally inquiring about comparable products which enhances the probability of a successful transaction. By employing search engine optimization (SEO), you can enhance the visibility of your online store and increase the likelihood that prospective consumers will encounter your products in search engine results.

People who look for information on the internet frequently begin their quest by using well-known search engines like Google or Bing.

These search engines are meant to filter through the varied material that can be found on websites and generate a ranked list of results according to the exact search queries that are entered. They first determine which websites have the greatest possibility of being relevant to the search query, and then they provide the results in the order of relevancy.

Search Results:

Your online store's prominence in search results may be affected by a number of factors, including the following:

- The percentage of a website's total traffic that comes from unpaid or organic sources, such as social media or other websites, which links to the website's storefront.

- The authority of your website, as measured by aspects such as the level of user engagement and other indicators that are pertinent.

- The number of years you've owned your domain name.

- Both the structure and the content of your website are improved so that they are friendlier to search engines.

It may be difficult for those who are just starting out in the world of online retail to have an immediate impact on the first three elements.

Developing a positive reputation for your company takes time and consistent effort, as does obtaining backlinks from other websites. On the other hand, with your content strategy, you can make plans for your long-term success.

Optimizing your content to make it more identifiable by search engines in relation to searches connected to your products is the most accessible approach to bring more traffic to your online store in the short term. This will help you sell more of the things you sell online.

This methodology is typically referred to as SEO, which stands for "search engine optimization."

To improve the search engine optimization of a website for an online store, there are a few fundamental strategies that need to be used.

Several examples of such strategies are presented in the following:

Find out what words and phrases consumers are entering into search engines to find goods and services similar to yours, and then capitalize on those. Which particular search terms are most effective in luring customers to shop at your establishment?

Creating Content:

When you are creating the content for your website, it is important to remember to add pertinent keywords in strategic locations such as the page titles, meta descriptions, and image alt text.

It is of the utmost importance to check that the URLs and file identifiers exactly match the content that is being shown on the screen.

By adding the whole domain to Google Search Console, you may increase the crawling and indexing rates of the website for your online business.

Blogs:

Integrating information that was derived from a blog into a website is a supplementary and efficient way to increase the amount of organic traffic that is delivered towards a website.

This strategy has the potential to enhance the amount of organic traffic that is sent to a website over an extended period of time, which may ultimately lead to an increase in sales. The blog publication and content generation tools that are included in the majority of e-commerce platforms can be put to effective use for a variety of purposes.

In the same way that maintaining your blog and optimizing your website for search engines are crucial, marketing is one of the most important factors that will determine the success of your online store.

The most effective marketing strategy is typically the one whose execution requires the fewest financial resources but still achieves the desired results.

Spreading postings on self-established social media platforms that are relevant to one's company and the things it sells is one feasible method that can be utilized to kick-start marketing attempts.

Social Media:

Establishing dedicated pages on well-known social media platforms such as Facebook and Instagram can be an efficient method for acquainting prospective customers with your company's offerings and increasing brand awareness.

Additionally, giving some thought to the creation of a YouTube channel is something you should do. Your product listings will be seen by more people if you share them in a thoughtful manner on Facebook groups that are relevant to your target audience, as well as on specialized free classified ad websites that cater to your particular market sector.

Marketing:

It is recommended that you give some thought to the manufacturing of business cards that provide a brief summary of your company as well as the URL of your online store. This will enable you to give the cards to anyone with whom you come into contact.

Additionally, it is highly recommended that you give some thought to posting flyers and other promotional materials for your organization on the bulletin boards that are typically found on college campuses.

Because marketing plays such a crucial part in drawing in and retaining a larger customer base, it is essential that a major emphasis be placed on this facet of the business. It is essential to keep in mind that the success of one's marketing efforts can have a direct influence on the amount of financial benefit one experiences.

If a person's website is already generating revenue, they should give some thought to the possibility of reinvesting some of that money in other forms of marketing activity if they want to continue growing their business.

Organizations now have the capacity to deploy focused advertising activities on several platforms, such as Google Ads and Facebook Ads, with the freedom to personalize these campaigns to correspond with their financial resources.

Examples of these platforms are Google and Facebook. The primary purpose of this endeavor is to increase the number of people who are familiar with and aware of your website who utilize the internet.

It is advisable to approach one's acquaintances without reluctance and request their assistance in advertising one's website, while also urging their connections to engage in similar acts.

This is the best course of action to take if one possesses acquaintances who have big followings or broad networks. Pyramid marketing, despite its seemingly modest look, has the ability to reach a huge number of persons, perhaps numbering in the hundreds or even millions.

This is because pyramid marketing works by encouraging participants to recruit others to participate in the scheme.

Customer Loyalty Benefits:

To encourage repeat business on your website, one useful method is to give loyal clients the opportunity to earn prizes for their continuous patronage of the company by presenting them with loyalty benefits. This strategy not only helps businesses keep their existing customers, but it also leads to higher revenues and a wider range of customer demographics.

Funnels:

The utilization of email funnels is another powerful tactic that should be taken into consideration. A marketing strategy known as an email funnel is a technique that was developed expressly to guide prospective consumers along a path that, in the end, results in those customers becoming purchasers. It is a methodical procedure that makes use of email correspondence to cultivate leads and turn them into paying clients.

Email funnels are constructed with a series of carefully produced emails that are designed to be sent in sequence. Each email serves a unique role within the context of the customer journey. The objective is to lead potential customers through a series of stages, beginning with the first awareness stage and ending with the conversion stage. At the very beginning of the sales process, the primary goals are to raise awareness of the brand and capture the interest of prospective clients. As the process goes on, it delves deeper into engagement, sparking curiosity, giving content that is engaging, and lastly encouraging conversion.

The execution of these funnels frequently depends heavily on the automation of email communications. It enables businesses to send relevant and timely communications to individuals based on their interactions with past emails or website behavior.

These interactions can be gleaned from the individual's history of interacting with websites or emails. Email funnels strive to optimize the possibility of turning prospects into satisfied purchasers by delivering good information, solving requirements, and offering offers in a smart manner.

An email funnel is essentially a dynamic marketing tool that directs prospects along a predetermined path. Because of this, it is an effective strategy for companies that want to increase the number of conversions they get and improve their relationships with customers.

CONCLUSION

In conclusion, "From Zero To E-Commerce Hero" by Abraham Wright presents a practical and actionable guide for anyone aspiring to achieve remarkable success in the world of e-commerce. As detailed in the five fundamental steps, this book demystifies the journey to building a multi-million-dollar online business with a budget as modest as $100 per month.

The journey begins by "Finding a Niche," where you learn to identify a market segment that aligns perfectly with your business goals. Next, "Finding a Local Supplier" is the key to securing the necessary inventory, setting the stage for your e-commerce venture. "Building an E-commerce Site or Cloning One" equips you with the essential tools to establish a digital presence that captures your audience's attention.

Once your foundation is set, you dive into "Getting the Price Right." Here, you gain the skills to set competitive and profitable pricing, a vital element in your journey to success. And finally, "SEO and Marketing Strategy" unveils the strategies and tactics needed to promote your business effectively and enhance your online visibility.
In a world where e-commerce can be a complex and daunting landscape, "From Zero To E-Commerce Hero" offers a clear and practical narrative, guiding you from zero to hero, where the promise of success is tangible, and the path is illuminated.

Whether you're just starting your e-commerce journey or looking to elevate your existing business, this book empowers you to seize the opportunity and chart your course toward e-commerce triumph. So, embark on this transformative journey, embrace these five essential steps, and script your own success story from zero to e-commerce hero.

The End